AF672083

CATHEDRAL CITIES OF ENGLAND

LECTOR HOUSE PUBLIC DOMAIN WORKS

This book is a result of an effort made by Lector House towards making a contribution to the preservation and repair of original classic literature. The original text is in the public domain in the United States of America, and possibly other countries depending upon their specific copyright laws.

In an attempt to preserve, improve and recreate the original content, certain conventional norms with regard to typographical mistakes, hyphenations, punctuations and/or other related subject matters, have been corrected upon our consideration. However, few such imperfections might not have been rectified as they were inherited and preserved from the original content to maintain the authenticity and construct, relevant to the work. The work might contain a few prior copyright references as well as page references which have been retained, wherever considered relevant to the part of the construct. We believe that this work holds historical, cultural and/or intellectual importance in the literary works community, therefore despite the oddities, we accounted the work for print as a part of our continuing effort towards preservation of literary work and our contribution towards the development of the society as a whole, driven by our beliefs.

We are grateful to our readers for putting their faith in us and accepting our imperfections with regard to preservation of the historical content. We shall strive hard to meet up to the expectations to improve further to provide an enriching reading experience.

Though, we conduct extensive research in ascertaining the status of copyright before redeveloping a version of the content, in rare cases, a classic work might be incorrectly marked as not-in-copyright. In such cases, if you are the copyright holder, then kindly contact us or write to us, and we shall get back to you with an immediate course of action.

HAPPY READING!

CATHEDRAL CITIES OF ENGLAND

WILLIAM WIEHE COLLINS

9 789356 146563
ISBN: 978-93-5614-656-3

Published: 1908

© 2022
LECTOR HOUSE LLP

LECTOR HOUSE

LECTOR HOUSE LLP
E-MAIL: info@lectorhouse.com

CATHEDRAL CITIES OF ENGLAND

60 REPRODUCTIONS FROM ORIGINAL WATERCOLORS

BY

W. W. COLLINS

1908

LIST OF ILLUSTRATIONS

BATH—PULTENEY BRIDGE

CANTERBURY—THE BAPTISTERY AND CHAPTER HOUSE

CANTERBURY—CHRISTCHURCH GATEWAY

CANTERBURY—INTERIOR OF THE NAVE

CANTERBURY—FROM THE MEADOWS

CANTERBURY—THE NORMAN STAIRWAY

CHESTER—THE ROWS

CHESTER—ST. WERBURGH STREET

CHESTER—BISHOP LLOYD'S PALACE AND WATERGATE STREET

CHESTER—EASTGATE STREET

CHICHESTER—FROM THE NORTHEAST

DURHAM—THE WESTERN TOWERS

DURHAM—FROM THE RAILWAY

DURHAM—INTERIOR OF CATHEDRAL LOOKING ACROSS THE NAVE INTO SOUTH TRANSEPT

DURHAM—ELVET BRIDGE

DURHAM—FRAMWELL GATE BRIDGE

ELY—FROM THE WEST FRONT

ELY—INTERIOR OF THE NAVE

ELY—FROM THE FENS

ELY—THE MARKET PLACE

EXETER—FROM THE PALACE GARDENS

EXETER—MOL'S COFFEE TAVERN

EXETER—INTERIOR OF THE NAVE

GLOUCESTER—THE CATHEDRAL AND OLD PARLIAMENT HOUSE

GLOUCESTER—FROM THE PADDOCK

GLOUCESTER—INTERIOR OF THE NAVE

HEREFORD—THE NORTH TRANSEPT

LONDON—ST. PAUL'S AND LUDGATE HILL

LONDON—WESTMINSTER ABBEY. THE NORTH TRANSEPT

LINCOLN—BY MOONLIGHT

LINCOLN—THE WEST TOWERS

LINCOLN—THE STEEP HILL

NORWICH—THE ÆTHELBERT GATE

NORWICH—THE MARKET PLACE

NORWICH—FROM THE NORTHEAST

OXFORD—CHRISTCHURCH GATEWAY

OXFORD—CHRISTCHURCH INTERIOR OF THE NAVE

PETERBOROUGH—THE WEST FRONT

PETERBOROUGH—THE MARKET PLACE

RIPON—THE CATHEDRAL

ROCHESTER—CATHEDRAL AND CASTLE

ST. ALBANS—FROM THE WALLS OF OLD VERULAM

SALISBURY—THE MARKET CROSS

SALISBURY—THE CATHEDRAL

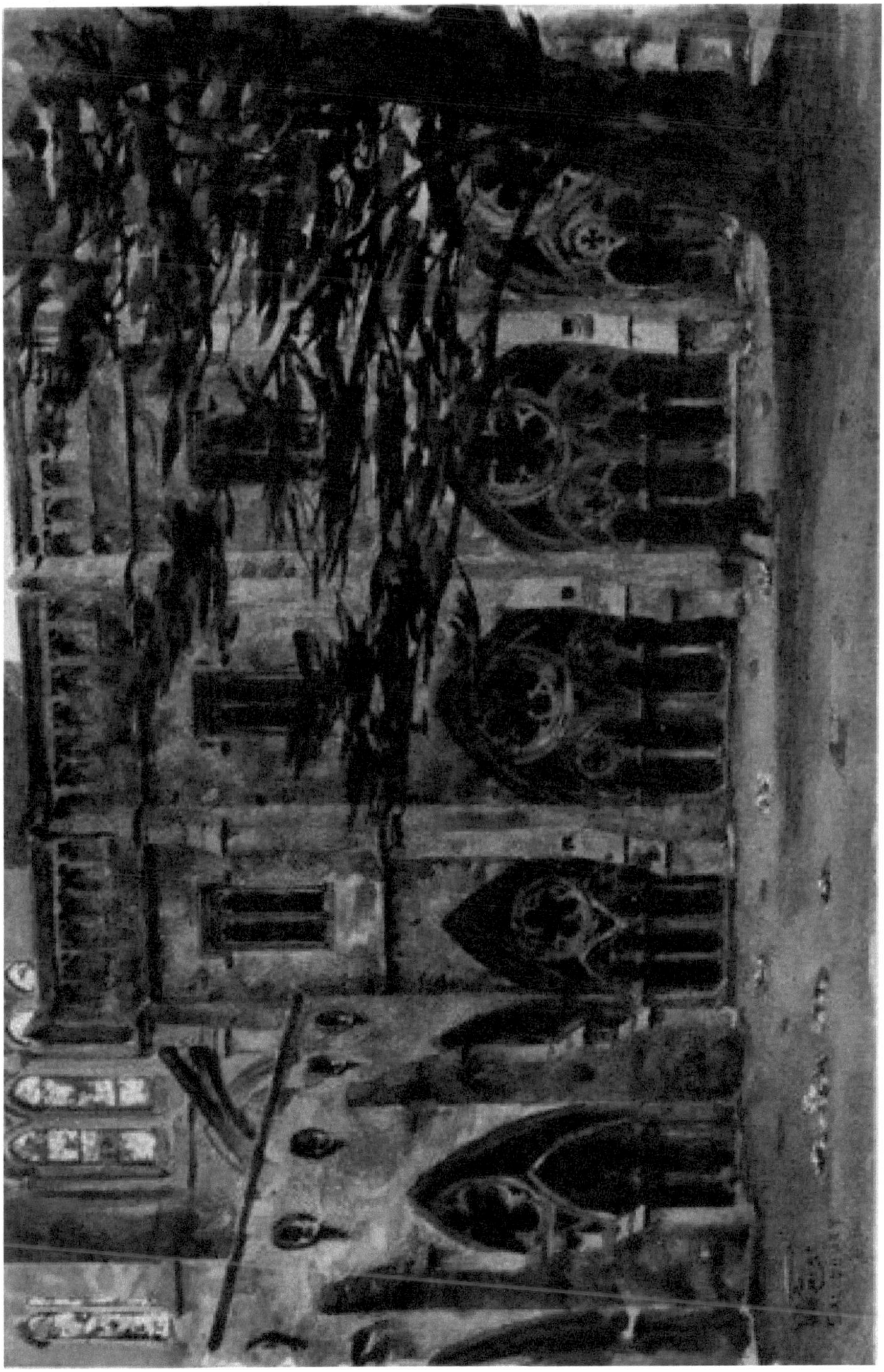

SALISBURY—THE CLOISTERS

SALISBURY—HIGH STREET GATEWAY INTO THE CLOSE

WINCHESTER—FROM THE DEANERY GARDEN

WINCHESTER—THE NORTH AISLE

WINCHESTER—ST. CROSS

WINCHESTER—FROM ST. CATHERINE'S HILL

WORCESTER—THE CATHEDRAL

WELLS—THE RUINS OF THE BANQUETING HALL

WELLS—CATHEDRAL AND THE POOLS

WELLS—FROM THE FIELDS

YORK—THE SHAMBLES

YORK—MICKLEGATE BAR

YORK—MONK BAR

LICHFIELD—THE WEST FRONT

YORK—BOOTHAM BAR

YORK—STONEGATE

Lector House believes that a society develops through a two-fold approach of continuous learning and adaptation, which is derived from the study of classic literary works spread across the historic timeline of literature records. Therefore, we aim at reviving, repairing and redeveloping all those inaccessible or damaged but historically as well as culturally important literature across subjects so that the future generations may have an opportunity to study and learn from past works to embark upon a journey of creating a better future.

This book is a result of an effort made by Lector House towards making a contribution to the preservation and repair of original ancient works which might hold historical significance to the approach of continuous learning across subjects.

HAPPY READING & LEARNING!

LECTOR HOUSE

LECTOR HOUSE LLP

E-MAIL: info@lectorhouse.com

9 789356 146563

9 789356 146563

Printed by Libri Plureos GmbH in Hamburg,
Germany